Hope Through It All

Hope Through It All

*Poems for the Ordinary, Tough, and
Beautiful Moments with God*

Naomi Brooks

RESOURCE *Publications* • Eugene, Oregon

HOPE THROUGH IT ALL
Poems for the Ordinary, Tough, and Beautiful Moments with God

Copyright © 2025 Naomi Brooks. All rights reserved. Except for brief quotations in critical publications or reviews, no part of this book may be reproduced in any manner without prior written permission from the publisher. Write: Permissions, Wipf and Stock Publishers, 199 W. 8th Ave., Suite 3, Eugene, OR 97401.

Resource Publications
An Imprint of Wipf and Stock Publishers
199 W. 8th Ave., Suite 3
Eugene, OR 97401

www.wipfandstock.com

PAPERBACK ISBN: 979-8-3852-5997-7
HARDCOVER ISBN: 979-8-3852-5998-4
EBOOK ISBN: 979-8-3852-5999-1

VERSION NUMBER 12/01/25

Scripture quotations taken from The Holy Bible, New International Version®, NIV®. Copyright © 1973, 1978, 1984, 2011 by Biblica, Inc. Used with permission of Zondervan. All rights reserved worldwide. www.zondervan.com.

"This book is thoughtful. A hand on the shoulder in the midst of transitions. Though our world feels as if it is caving in—together we mount up with wings like eagles. *Hope Through It All* by Naomi Brooks is the epitome of this."

—**Michelle Olabode**, author of *Birds Sing in the Morning*

"We are deeply encouraged by Naomi Brooks's courage to express faith so authentically and creatively. In *Hope Through It All*, her words speak directly to the hearts of a generation learning to trust God through life's ordinary and stretching moments. Each poem carries the honesty of real faith and the hope that only Christ can give. Through her heartfelt poetry, Naomi captures the beauty of walking with God through both the waiting and the wonder. This collection uplifts, challenges, and reminds readers that God is present and working, even when life doesn't go to plan."

—**Bukunmi and Jumoke Olukoya**, Leaders, Impact Mission UK

"*Hope Through It All* by Naomi Brooks is a beautiful and intentional collection that speaks to the heart with honesty and tenderness. Her words hold space for pain, healing, faith, and growth in a way that feels deeply personal, and yet so familiar. Reading this is a chance to feel seen, comforted, and reminded that hope is not just a feeling, but a choice we return to again and again. This book is for anyone who has had to keep going in the middle of life's uncertainty and is still choosing to believe in light. Naomi writes with sincerity, softness, and spiritual depth . . . the kind of poetry that sits with you long after you close the book."

—**Renee Kapuku**, Co-Founder, To My Sisters

Beautifully and masterfully written. Naomi weaves nature into neat and impressive lines on a page. In doing so she encourages us to not only read them, but let them wash over us, let them serve as a mirror as they reflect the changing seasons in our lives. In *Hope Through It All*, Naomi implores us as the reader to look in and self-reflect; look around at the evergreen love in many forms around us; and most importantly look above to our Heavenly Father who truly is our ever-present hope through it all, through every season."

—**Kezia Karunwi**, author of *Lessons From the Garden*

These poems were not created in isolation. They were given; breathed into life by God and carried forward by the love of those around me.

So, to my community—
For reading early drafts,
Offering your honest thoughts,
Reminding me of the vision God placed on my heart,
And encouraging me every step of the way . . .

With all my heart, *thank you.*

Contents

Preface | ix

1. For the planes of life with God
   - Figuring it all out (P.S. we all are) | 3
   - They said to twenty somethings | 4
   - Don't be afraid if your plans don't go to plan | 5
   - I don't want to move out | 7
   - With friends | 9
   - I hope love finds me | 10
   - Falling in love on accident | 11
   - Don't let fear stop you | 12

2. For when suffering surfaces and the waves hit
   - Some things, take time | 15
   - God works it out for good | 16
   - Destined for God's goodness | 17
   - Springs of water | 18
   - Please, Father | 19
   - I'm waiting and awaiting | 20
   - Wade and trust | 22
   - Encourage our hearts | 23
   - For a hard season | 24

3. For when God gives us the strength to hold on
   - Get up nine | 27
   - Hope is infectious | 29
   - There will be a time to start again | 30
   - I remember God | 31

If you find me | 33
Your goodness abounds | 34
Sometimes missteps | 35
Resilient hope | 38
The oak tree | 39

4 For when God makes it all beautiful in time
Faithful Father | 43
You are valued | 44
God is faithful | 46
Joy of the Lord | 47
Accept it | 48
Blessings in this season | 50
May you come to know | 51
Good plans | 52
Better than you expect | 53
Reflecting on a love that I don't deserve | 54
You are important to God | 55
If you dared to sing | 56

Preface

God gave me these poems in the quiet stretches of ordinary days, in the shadowed depths of the valleys, and on the bright heights of the mountaintops.

In every place, He reminded me that He has never forgotten me, that He has never overlooked how I feel, and that He is always with me. He is working all things together for good, shaping me more and more into the image of His Son (Romans 8:28-29).

These poems encouraged me to have *hope through it all*, even in the hardest seasons. My prayer is that as you read them, they will also encourage you to hold on to hope and believe that His faithful hand is at work in your own story.

Love,
Nae x

Chapter 1
For the planes of life with God

Romans 5:1-2 (NIV)

Therefore, since we have been justified through faith, we have peace with God through our Lord Jesus Christ, ² through whom we have gained access by faith into this grace in which we now stand. And we boast in the hope of the glory of God.

Figuring it all out (P.S. we all are)

Not yet thirty,
But your teens are through,
You're starting to wonder,
If you've found the real you.

Friendships evolving,
Relationships building,
Things are changing,
But somehow stay same-ing?

Nurturing your interests,
Figuring out the world,
All that is within you,
Is being unfurled.

Blooming and glowing,
In both difficulties and delights—
You're twenty-something,
Figuring out life.

They said to twenty somethings

Graduate from university / Or do an apprenticeship — *something* my dear / Have fun but not too much / Graduate with at least a two one / Make sure you join a society committee, for your LinkedIn bio / Find a job immediately, so you have a good answer for 'what's next' / Heaven forbid you leave without a boyfriend / (Even though they told you don't date until you're 21) / Stay at home to save / But not for too long! / Rent. / But don't rent with friends, or people you don't know / Buy. / But don't buy a flat, buy a house in the middle of nowhere and commute / Get your driving licence, especially you Londoners who have TfL / Buy a car / But don't get a loan / Enjoy being single / But not too much—gotta be ready to mingle and be ever ready to meet the right person / Travel the world! / But don't overdo it / But don't do the most / *But—*

But maybe we should be saying this instead? . . .

They should *say to twenty somethings:*

Study something you love or see value in / Trust in God and do your best with and for Him / Embrace all that your season has to bring / Don't let fear stop you / You don't always have to be the loudest in the room / But don't be afraid to take up space / Be thoughtful about what you want to do next / Hope for the best and be wise / Network and make connections / Invest in friendships and relationships / Invest in yourself / Invest in understanding money / Don't be afraid to fail / Try new things / Learn about yourself / Learn about God / Learn and soak it all up / Bloom—

Pierce the earth, say hello to the sun and rise into all God has created you to be.

Don't be afraid if your plans don't go to plan

I know sometimes,
we can make our plans,
make meticulous lists with,
intricate intermediate steps.
Diligently work it out,
and *still*,
our plans don't go to plan.

I know sometimes,
we can chart our path,
outline our journey, and
the steps we need to take.
Doing our best to eradicate,
the possibility for mistakes,
and *still*,
our journeys go awry.

I know sometimes,
we can figure it out,
make the call, set the meeting,
open the business account.
Feeling the fear and doing it anyway,
and *still*,
the vision doesn't crystallize.

But I know always,
amidst planning, moving . . .
God is perfecting our paths,
lighting up our steps.
So even in our doubt and fear,
He *still*
Is working it all out for *good*.

I don't want to move out

No, I don't want to move out.
But I kinda do.
I dream of lazy mornings,
without doors swinging open,
with a question about where I've put the door stop (?!)
Now uncompromisingly awake,
alas my lie-in dream,
like the dream I was sharply awoken from,
is over.

So, yeah, I do want to move out.
But I kinda don't.
I value the safety, the reliability, the familiarity.
Ordered items with designated places,
knowledge of shortcuts and side roads,
and the alleys to avoid,
back streets that get me on my way,
quickly does it . . .
Home-cooked food.

So, I don't want to move out.
But I do.
I feel it: the growth, the maturity, the independence,
and the fact that I would be good at living on my own.

In many ways, I've already left the nest,
and this next step is the actualization,
of the leader inside of me.

So, I do want to move out.
But I don't.
I love my family, their quirks and unconditional love . . .
To say the least, goodbye will yield pain.
But I yearn for fertile soil,
that can be a home for seeds inside of me—
seeds that have been waiting too long to sprout their roots . . .
and reach up into the new.
If I stay too long,
could I miss my peak?

So, I will move out.
But when?
Is it now, is it later?
Alone, or together?
Do I rent, do I buy?
Is it fear, that I haven't tried?
Twenty-something, but still a girl,
and going out, into the world.
About to spread, my beautiful wings;
    to fly
        and soar
            to glide
                and sing.

With friends

Shared secrets over sweet tea; Gluttonous guffaws that hurt tummies; Tears caught on shoulders; Arms wrapped around, with palms gently rubbing the back of your cotton t-shirt; Elbows engaged as you walk through the city; Gazes locked with love or laughter shared—*What beauty in wordless conversation/s;* Expressions matched as the bass drops; Honest opinions, even if it hurts; Glasses raised in pride; Real moments.

With friends.

I hope love finds me

I hope love finds me.
I hope it whistles in the wind.
I hope it settles like pebble droplets
on dark green sheaves,
and waits.
I hope it meets me as the sun rays do;
streaming through my window
on summer mornings.
I hope it sits like cotton candy
on the open skies,
beckoning me to be still,
and enjoy.
I hope it hides me, like tree branches do
when it's pouring ropes of rain.
I hope love finds me in the ordinarily beautiful;
the supremely normal;
the everyday and mundane.
I hope it finds me in every moment.
And I hope it finds you too.

Falling in love on accident

I never thought I'd fall in love,
I never thought he'd catch me,
This love I feel has always been,
A dreamy dream I'd fancy.

But then one day he did appear;
My fancy dream grew wings.
It flapped and flew and bloomed and grew,
Until the bird could sing.

Songs of care and deep support,
Songs that show I'm loved.
Reminders every single day,
Reflecting God above.

This love I feel, I feel deep down,
Deep down right in my bones.
This love I feel, I feel deep down,
Deep down, right to my toes.
This love I feel, I feel deep down,
It settles me to rest.
This love I feel, I feel deep down,
Is God's very best.

Don't let fear stop you

Don't let fear stop you:
Don't let timidity get in your way.

Don't let fear stop you:
Through it all, you have access to His grace.

Don't let fear stop you:
You can always trust the Ancient of Days.

Don't let fear stop you:
Like Joshua, God is with you always.

Chapter 2

For when suffering surfaces and the waves hit

Romans 5:3a (NIV)
Not only so, but we also glory in our sufferings

Some things, take time

My mind is racing,
My heart cries, *"What's next?"*
My hope is fading,
All I feel is regret.

Yet, God is doing,
Something, unseen;
Some things,
Take time,
To come,
Into being.

God works it out for good

As the tears wash my face, and
I mourn what didn't come true,
My heart looks for comfort:
It focusses on You.

Your Word will never fail,
You're my peace, and hope too,
Good things are still planned,
As I lie in wait of You.

Destined for God's goodness

Though it seems bleak, and
Our hard hearts crave more,
May we choose the road,
Less travelled, and trust,
In the Lord.

Though we have begun,
To believe the lies,
May we let God's Word,
Infuse our hearts, and
Heal our minds.

For sure we will faint,
Unless we believe,
That God's goodness is,
Destined for us to,
Taste and see.

Springs of water

May springs of water, bourgeon forth relentlessly in this seemingly barren desert.

May springs become streams of hope and faith in your heart, nurturing seeds of character and purpose unseen.

May springs keep your focus fixed on believing, being and becoming who God made you to be.

May springs dull the unrelenting aches of pain and yearning, creating deep wells rich with patience,

As we wait.

Please, Father

Please hold my hand Father,
Life doesn't make sense.

I'm scared, worried, confused,
And truly, I'm spent.

Fear is running my mind,
I'm struggling to rest.

I really need a shift right now,
Life is putting me to the test.

Dear, don't you know I'm with you?
You don't have to be afraid.

I'm preparing the best for you,
I haven't led you astray.

Waiting makes you stronger,
It builds character and faith.

Even in the valley of death,
I'm beside you always.

I'm waiting and awaiting

I'm waiting
Awaiting
The reveal of Your promise.

I'm hoping
And yearning
The passing of prophecy.

I'm looking
I'm seeking
Confirmation all 'round me.

And I'm waiting
Awaiting
Terrified that I heard wrong.

I keep waiting
Awaiting
And keep on strengthening my faith.

And I'm choosing
To keep losing
The idol of my own way.

You are crafting
And molding
Me into my truest self.

And I'm cherishing
The changing
As I hold on to You more.

Yes, I'm waiting
Awaiting
More confidence and trust in You.

Yes, I'm faith-ing
And enduring
What You have called me into.

But in seeking
And praying
I've still a misstep or two.

I'm believing
And trusting
And knowing
And hoping
That through Your
Loyal loving
You'll work it out for good.

Wade and trust

Wade in the water,
Wade in the waiting,
He's present here, loved one,
Trust His leading.

Encourage our hearts

Sometimes
In the darkest night
All I,
Better still,
We
Can do is encourage our hearts.

May it be
A silent prayer
A song of praise
A shout of hope
A song of faith

No matter how, or when
May we have the courage
To encourage
Our hearts

As we wait.

For a hard season

God, I look to You
And Your promises
As You ask me to
Be patient and wait.

I will remember
Those who wait on God
Will renew their strength
And they will not faint.

For when You know the
Father's heart for You
And when You know that
He does want Your best.

Then You can trust Him.
Hold on to His Word.
For this hard season
Will leave You blessed.

Chapter 3

For when God gives us the strength to hold on

Romans 5:3b–4 (NIV)

because we know that suffering produces perseverance; perseverance, character; and character, hope.

Get up nine

This morning, I looked out of my window,
and realized . . . it's spring:

> The burgeoning bluebells in bloom,
>> blazing with brilliance, and delight.

> Pink-petaled petunias peeking out,
>> with promise of something new.

> Red roses rising resplendently,
>> beckoning you to gaze.

> Wildflowers waving in the wind,
>> welcoming you to rest.

> Sunflowers, yellow and bright,
>> sparkling in the sunlight.

Yes, it's Spring.

Reminding us,
another year,
there is beauty,
where there was once . . .
nothing.

Reminding us,
that if you sow,
and if you prune,
and if you wait . . .
true beauty can . . .
take hold.

Reminding us,
that tomorrow,
you can still bloom,
in unabashed,
beauty.

Reminding us,
to get back up,
to not stay down,
to rise and shine—
reminding us,
that we can fall,
even eight times . . .
    And get up nine.

Hope is infectious

Hope is infectious.
Little by little,
It seeps in,
It ebbs and flows,
And slowly changes,
The sinews of your heart.
Sweeping away the tears of,
your once-weeping heart.
Transforming you,
Into a hopeful you,
A smiling and shining you.

Dearly beloved,
How I missed you.

There will be a time to start again

Every autumn
Deciduous trees
Lose their leaves
And let go of rich green
To proudly proclaim
Bare branches.

And take
time out
to rest.

So, they
can give
their best.

In the quiet
Embracing the still
They gather strength
And hopes to fulfil
With gusto and beauty
In spring.

I remember God

Sometimes I try to hide my flaws.
And run for cover,
Burrowing myself in my sheets,
Closing my eyes tight,
Willing myself to forget.

Or I try to bury them,
I dig deep and,
Collect all the soil I can possibly find,
Cover them until all that can be seen is a mound of earth.

Sometimes I run from them,
Letting go of stationary hiding,
My legs carry me along as I twist and turn in the maze of me,
Forbidding myself to turn back and look.

But then I remember God.

I remember that I am more than my flaws.
I remember that someone has seen them all,
and still chooses to love and bless me.

What does that mean?
If the almighty, perfect God reckons with the worst part of me,
and loves me, regardless . . .
What say me?

What say you?

So, I walk back to face them . . .
I push back the soil,
And I open up the covers,
And my eyes,
To see me.

And I do see flaws.
But I also see beauty,
And opportunity to become even more.

So, I choose to love myself.

For who I am,
and who I am becoming,
For His glory.

If you find me

If you find me,
Sitting at the riverside, my toes pointed, gently moving
　as the waves oscillate,
My hands gently rustling the tufts of grass blades underneath
　my palms,
My eyes locked on the coral sunset that paints the skies
　splendidly . . .
Know this.

I have found quiet for my soul, for just a moment,
And peace has risen to meet me.
For I am beholding the beauty of the world God created for us.
And I am taking
Just a moment
To, in fact, seek
And find Him.

Your goodness abounds

Lord, let my life,
Bring beams of light,
So that joy shines forth,
Through the depths of night.

Through life's ups and downs,
Your goodness abounds.
So let hope and faith,
In my life, resound.

Sometimes missteps

Sometimes missteps
aren't really missed steps.
Sometimes missteps
are new avenues
that you
would only choose
by missing
'attractive' routes.

Maybe your failures
of the past
aren't going to
leave you last.
And God's miraculous movements
are ushering you
into
the prepared road ahead.

Sometimes
the road looks paved
and sometimes
it looks rough.

Sometimes
it's meandering meadows
and sometimes
old grass with aged tufts,
that stretch you
and transform you
on the journey to
the real you.

The person who
can sustain the destiny
at hand.

The person who
will not just land,
but expand.

Maybe the greatness
you're meant for
requires you to
stumble, trip
a few times.

Maybe a little
failure and missteps
are necessary,
so that what is necessary
isn't missed
by premature steps
in a fake mission
and sour limelight.

I say this all to encourage you to:
Trust God's leading and beautiful timing.

He is an intentional and trustworthy Father.

Resilient hope

I am hopeful: for what's to come, for what is, for what has left me.

Hopeful that it will be beautiful.

Hopeful that even today I can see God's goodness . . . in even the smallest of ways.

Hopeful that God's plan will continue to unfold and unfurl gloriously, as my character blooms.

The oak tree

If you'd look at the oak tree,
Majestic and strong,
You would realize that growth,
Can take quite long.

Every part of that tree allows it,
To stand tall, today.
I wonder if we could,
Learn from that, some way?

Sometimes I wonder,
How long was I a seed?
How long was I a baby?
How long was I in need?

How much did I rely on
Others to feed me?
How much did I learn so I,
Could rely on me?

Sometimes I wonder,
How long was I a root?
How long did it take me,
To steady and shoot?

'Cause shooting for the stars ain't,
For the faint of heart.
Deep and resilient roots,
Are needed to start.

So, in every season,
Take time to discern,
What God wants you to,
Understand and learn.

It may not bring pleasure,
You may bear some weight.
But the oak tree reminds us,
Growth is worth the wait.

Chapter 4

For when God makes it all beautiful in time

Romans 5:5 (NIV)

And hope does not put us to shame, because God's love has been poured out into our hearts through the Holy Spirit, who has been given to us.

Faithful Father

A faithful Father,
A precious King.
The One who knows both,
Your best and sin.

He knows your flaws,
And loves you too,
His faithful heart is,
Committed to you.

You are valued

Today, God reminded me,
of His love and His care,
That today and forever,
His presence will be here.

Guiding and leading,
Forgiving and comforting,
His dear, special child,
Who He is in endless wanting.

He did the unthinkable,
To meet me in my need,
So I rest in the truth of who,
He created me to be.

So, step out! Be bold!
Be courageous and fear not!
For God still sees you,
Never you, has He forgot.

Say yes to the confidence,
His Spirit gives to you,
And walk in the knowledge,
That God is for you.

No more sadness and weeping,
Thinking God doesn't care,
He loves you and created you,
For now, for right here.

Before I finish,
I'll say again: you are loved,
Adored and cherished
By the One above.

I'm in awe of His love,
That is being revealed to me:
The width, the length, the height, the depth ...
May we *all* see.

God is faithful

God is faithful
In all His ways
All your days
He is faithful.

God is faithful
In the big and small
Through it all
He is faithful.

God is faithful
When you are down
In Him you're found
He is faithful.

God is faithful
Keep holding on
In Him you're strong
He is faithful.

Joy of the Lord

Let joy run like a river,
Let there be goodness,
Ever more.
Let peace saturate my soul,
Let love rain; let love pour.

Accept it

God is reckless in His love for you,
God is reckless in His pursuit,
God is committed to being there for you,
Let these words take root,

God shouts it from the mountaintops,
How much He loves you and cares,
Don't just take my Word for it,
Check the Word of God—it's there.

For God so loved the world, it says,
In John three, sixteen,
That He laid down his life and sacrificed,
It all for you and me.

The greatest love known to man,
Is where life is laid down,
God did this for you! Be rest assured,
He loves you, here and now.

No need to fear if you're good enough,
You're of immense value to Him,
From the beginning of time, He made up His mind,
And His love will never dim.

You are precious; you are imago Dei,
When God sees you, He sees Himself,
Like a mother who can't turn her son away,
Only to love you, is His heart is compelled.

You were chosen and are royalty,
Before you were, God knew your name,
He's crowned you with beauty and majesty,
But do you see yourself the same?

A fearfully and wonderfully made creation,
Yes, you are! Through and through,
Every hair on your head is considered by God,
Accept it—He adores *you*.

Blessings in this season

I pray You give me eyes to see,
Not just the goodness you are preparing for me . . .
But also, the
Blessings
That are here and now.
For joy
and love
and peace,
In this season,
Abound.

May you come to know

May you come to know
A love so high it pushes past the clouds,

May you come to feel
A love so deep it's ten thousand feet into the ground,

May you come to hear
A love so loud it ripples in your soul,

May you come to know
The truest love: God's love that makes you whole.

Good plans

You're made fearfully,
And wonderfully—
Intentionally too.

He knows every hair,
On your head, dear child.
God has good planned for you.

Better than you expect

But is it not true, that just for you,
God prepared beauty,
That is ready to bloom?

But is it not true, that just for you,
Blessings are stocked,
And love is too?

But is it not true, that just for you,
God's heart is forever,
Turned towards you?

So is it not true, that just for you,
God is going to do better,
Than you expect Him to?

Reflecting on a love that I don't deserve

God's grace surrounds you,
Reaching and searching,
Yearning to bless you,
When not deserving.

His beautiful heart,
Abounds in mercy,
Commits to loving,
When we are messy.

What love is this,
That my worst is pardoned,
My sins forgiven,
And my best hoped in?

May I live a life that,
Gives thanks to Jesus,
The wonderful Savior,
Whose deep love has freed us.

You are important to God

His creation and masterpiece,
Before you were, He knew you,
For sure, more than anyone,
He's planned the best for you.

If you dared to sing

Do you see how the flowers grow,
Unabashed and with wonder?
With no doubt that they're accepted,
With no doubt of their splendor.

Do you see how the river runs,
And boldly takes up space?
Meandering and spreading,
In every direction and place.

Do you see how the fire burns,
And is willing to consume?
It is regal in its majesty,
You have no choice but to make room.

Do you see how the birds tweet,
Every morning without fail?
Whether sleeping lids or bright eyes,
We experience their unique tale.

Nature knows it's accepted,
Nature knows it's loved by God,
Nature grabs hold of that freedom,
And to His glory,
Nature sings its song.

Its song to dance like fire,
Its song to tweet at daybreak,
Its song to splash forever,
Its song to shoot and shake.

I wonder what you would do,
If you received His immense love.

Knowing you are created,
In the image of God above.

Would you be,
fearless, resilient and purposeful,
in every octave of your song?

If you dared to sing,
would you discover the person,
who's been hidden in you all along?

www.ingramcontent.com/pod-product-compliance
Lightning Source LLC
Chambersburg PA
CBHW071415040426
42444CB00009B/2255